Del Mar Days
*Community Life and Civic Engagement
in a Small American City*

Combined 3 Book Overview
& Preview of Contents

Del Mar Days

Community Life and Civic Engagement in a Small American City

*A memoir, social history, and sourcebook
formed by commentaries in newspaper columns
about life and politics in the City of Del Mar, California
during the sparkling years between 1982 and 1995*

By
Eugene G. Schwartz

With a Foreword by
Greg Dennis

Combined 3 Book Overview
& Preview of Contents

Consortium House
Del Mar, California

Designed by Louie Neiheisel
Edited and indexed by Linnea Dayton

Copyright 2016 Eugene G. Schwartz

Published by Consortium House
693 Orchid Lane
Del Mar, CA 92014

http://bit.ly/DelMarDays
http://www.worthyshorts.com/Consortium/bookshop.html
http://delmarhistoricalsociety.org/bulletins/DelMarDaysBook.pdf

The columns and many of the photos in this book
appeared in
the *Del Mar Surfcomber*, Del Mar, California and
the *North County Blade-Citizen*, Solana Beach, California
during the years 1982–1995.

The author's *Surfcomber* and *Blade-Citizen* editors
during those years:
Greg Dennis, Rory Bennett,
Phil Urbina, Jim Trageser

Photo credits appear with individual images or are listed in Book 3.
Photos not credited are those of the author.

Produced and distributed for Consortium House
by CustomWorthy Editions
www.CustomWorthy.com

The Set: ISBN 978-0-9802161-0-3
CHP104
Book 1: ISBN 978-0-9802161-1-0
CHP105
Book 2: ISBN 978-0-9802161-2-7
CHP106
Book 3: ISBN 978-0-9802161-3-4
CHP107
Combined 3 Book Overview & Preview of Contents
CHP108: ISBN 978-0-9802161-4-1

Printed in the United States of America

To Nancy Ewing,
Madam Del Mar

"Where the love is"

And to
Dick Roe, Publisher
Herb Turner, Artist and Builder

"Citizens engaged."

With gratitude and appreciation for the support of
the Del Mar Historical Society,
And in fond memory of the Society's founder
H. K. "Swede" Throneson

Publication of Del Mar Days
has been made possible through the generosity of
an initial grant from donors
who wish to remain anonymous,
and additional funding from (partial list):
Sam Borgese
The Warren Family Foundation

Colorful hot-air balloons provide a complete view of Del Mar's 2.5-mile coastline, fairgrounds and racetrack. Leading down from the bluffs at the north end of the beach, the sandy path shown at the left is one of the walking tour treats that I have enjoyed many times.

Overview: Books 1, 2 & 3

BOOK 1: PEOPLE & EVENTS

Overview: Books 1, 2 & 3

Foreword

Preface

About Book 1

Book 1 Contents

Part 1—Celebrations & Remembrances *(45 columns)*

Part 2—Del Mar Days *(48 columns)*

Scrapbook: The Way It Was *(14 two-page pictorials)*

Index to Book 1

BOOK 2: LAND USE, PUBLIC POLICY & LIBERTY

Overview: Books 1, 2 & 3

About Book 2

Book 2 Contents

Part 3—On Land and Its Uses *(49 columns)*

Part 4—Public Policy and the Neighborhood *(36 columns)*

Part 5—The Individual, Liberty, and Community *(41 columns)*

Afterword: The Big Debates *(12 columns)*

Epilog: Leaving Del Mar *(3 columns)*

Index to Book 2

BOOK 3: CITY OF DREAMS

Overview: Books 1, 2 & 3

About Book 3

Book 3 Contents

Part 6—City of Dreams *(9 columns)*

Excerpts & Commentaries

- 1. Cityhood Reconsidered and the 1960 Master Plan • 2. The Community Plan—1976
- 3. The San Dieguito Lagoon—1979 Resource Enhancement Program • 4. Del Mar 2000—1981
- 5. The Library and Civic Center Master Plan—1990–1992 • 6. The Local Coastal Land Use Plan—1993
- 7. The Garden—Del Mar - 2008 • 8. Design Review & Floor Area Ratio 1967–1992
- 9. The Ties That Bind—Del Mar and its Railroad 1882–1993

Bibliography and Commentary

Acknowledgments

Sources: Illustrations and Citations

Chronological List of Columns in Books 1, 2 & 3

Combined Index to Books 1, 2 & 3

Pictorials

BOOK 1

Frontispieces
Balloons Over Del Mar
Powerhouse Park—A Place for Remembering

Part 1
The Way It Was: Celebrations & Remembrances
Tom Pearson
The J. David Affair
Del Marriage
H. K. "Swede" & Marge Throneson
Lew & Ruby Hopkins

Part 2
The Way It Was: Del Mar Days
The Del Mar–Solana Beach Optimists
The Alvarado House

Scrapbook
The Way It Was: A Gallery of People, Events & Places
The Plaza: A Jewel in the Crown
The Inn L'Auberge
Thriving and Enterprising Community Theaters
Channel 37/38 Cable Provides a Stage
Richard Carter and the Arts Park
A Center for Publishers, Editors, and Designers
The Restaurateurs
Nancy Ewing: Madam Del Mar
Don McQuiston
Herb Turner
"Helen"—H. Montgomery-Drysdale
Alice Goodkind
Where the Surf Meets the Turf
The Canyon and the Lagoon

BOOK 2

Frontispieces
Del Mar Days—1983
Seagrove Park Twilight Concerts—1984

Part 3
The Way It Was: On Land & Its Uses
Jim & Carol Watkins
Jan McMillan

Part 4
The Way It Was: Public Policy & the Neighborhood
Dick Roe

Part 5
The Way It Was: The Individual, Liberty & Community
Pat Barnett

Afterword
The Way It Was: The Big Debates

Leaving Del Mar
The Way It Was: Del Mar & Woodstock Compared

BOOK 3

Frontispieces
Del Mar Centennial—1985
Keep Greenery in the Scenery—1972

Part 6
The Way It Was: City of Dreams & Rise of the Habitat
Bud Emerson

Back of the Book
Hotdance—1990
Del Mar Triathlon—1981
Innovations. Published!—1970

Preface

Small town life is a showcase for the compact among individuals that makes social order and self-realization possible. These are conditions not automatically guaranteed by nature, nor by each of us to the other. Once discovered, they need constantly to be reaffirmed.

This collection of columns, covering a period from 1982 to 1995, are in a way commentaries on the condition of social order and liberty in one small town, a 1.8-square-mile city, of 4,900–5,200 population at the time, on the coast of California, just north of San Diego.

The subtitle of the work, *Community Life and Civic Engagement in a Small American City*, points to my thematic focus. Namely, that out of many individual lives, stories, and events we can find not only the threads that make up our social history, but the energies that give life to our Republic. The threads and energies I have picked up in this work are not theoretical—they come from life as I have lived it.

The character of small town and neighborhood life tells us in intimate ways about who we are and what we expect of ourselves. Those were the lessons I learned as a consequence of the platform as a columnist that I enjoyed.

Especially I want to salute the book-publishing, arts, newspaper, and business communities in Del Mar that provided me with professional and social connection. And, equally, the environmental community. It provided both the commitment and the pushback that helped keep Del Mar's people and its magnificent beach, bluffs, canyons, and lagoon in as close to balance as pristine nature and the modern world could accommodate.

For a taste of what we argued about, fought over, and celebrated, take a walk along the beach from Scripps Bluffs to Torrey Pines State Reserve, and on the bluffs along the tracks. Walk up through the amazing Crest Canyon preserve, and on San Dieguito Drive along the Lagoon, and on 15th Street past the Rock Haus into the hills, and look north and south from the Plaza on Camino Del Mar and watch the richly hued sunsets.

Many dedicated, engaged, and gifted people in Del Mar made the experiences of which I wrote possible. Because this is a memoir as well as a documentary, of necessity it is a reflection of my own interests and point of view. Consequently, if I have failed anyone in this writing now or then, it was and is unintended and deeply regretted.

My dear friend Nancy Ewing, to whom I have dedicated this work, liked to say that "Del Mar is where the love is." As a transplanted boy from the Bronx, Del Mar became that place for me.

This is my tribute.

Gene Schwartz
Del Mar, California
January, 2016

About Book 1

In some of the columns in **Book 1**, I drew profiles of residents, civic leaders, artists, builders, and business people who defined the city, and I celebrated their holidays—these 45 columns are assembled in **Part 1**. They were written during the heyday of battles to preserve Del Mar's residential character as laid out in its 1976 Community Plan, and the years embracing its 1985 Centennial Celebration. In this small city, I wrote about relationships between city management, local businesses, residents, and civic leaders that were often close, personal, and intertwined—sharing joys and sorrows, holidays such as Christmas, July 4th, Thanksgiving, Rosh Hashanah, and Passover, as well as natural beauty and politics.

The 48 columns in **Part 2** of Book 1 focus on the years before and after the city's 1985 Centennial, when Del Mar experienced the flourishing and the later waning of local performance and graphic arts, street entertainments, and the publishing of books, periodicals, and training materials, many of which I worked with and wrote about.

At one point more than 300 people were employed in and around town by *Psychology Today* magazine and its book division, attracting an additional cadre of nationally recognized writers, graphic artists, editors, and other book professionals. Also, since the city hosted an Amtrak station a stone's throw from one of the few easily accessed and pristine beaches on the west coast, and a popular state fair and racetrack, Del Mar was not wanting for diversions on which I could columnize.

The columns assembled here chronicle the city's vibrant spontaneous cultural life, as it evolved into a comfortable menu of events that continue until this day.

In the **Scrapbook** section, a collection of photos and ephemera recalls some of the people, events, and themes that stand out in my memory and that I covered during my years as a columnist. They helped define the community: the Plaza, the Inn, the restaurateurs, the publishers and designers, the community theaters, local cable television, Richard Carter's Arts Park, historian Nancy Ewing, builder and artist Herb Turner, graphic designer Don McQuiston, photographer Helen Drysdale, environmentalist and artist Alice Goodkind, the racetrack, the state fair, the beach, lagoon, canyons, and bluffs. Part opener pages and individual pictorial pages elsewhere in the book add to the array.

Powerhouse Park:
A Place for Remembering

Two sentinel palms *(above)* flanked* "Nancy Ewing's bench" overlooking the Del Mar beach just north of the Poseidon and Jake's restaurants in 1992. Just to the right is the old Del Mar Hotel Powerhouse and its famous stack, which replaced the original 1909 structure in 1938.

Following late 1980s construction of Powerhouse Park, citizen efforts led to the Powerhouse Restoration Committee and the graciously remodeled community center, opened in 1999 (lower right).

Powerhouse Park is one of my favorite places to visit. Over your shoulder you may hear concerts in the park. Amtrak and commuter rail trains to the west race by along the bluffs, to and from San Diego and Los Angeles.

*The bench has since been removed and replaced.

City of Del Mar in 1975

This map appears on page 42 of the Community Plan as adopted by the voters of Del Mar in March 1976. It has been enhanced to show the land-use designations in color, to identify landmarks, and to sharpen street lines and names for legibility. During the 1980s the city's border was extended northward to encompass all of the Via de la Valle roadway. Also, Jimmy Durante Blvd. and Turf Rd. were consolidated to follow the bold line shown on the map.

KEY TO OPEN SPACE LANDMARKS

1. Scripps (North) Bluffs
2. San Dieguito Lagoon and river mouth
3. Seagrove Park
4. Crest Canyon
5. Anderson Canyon
6. Torrey Pines State Reserve extension

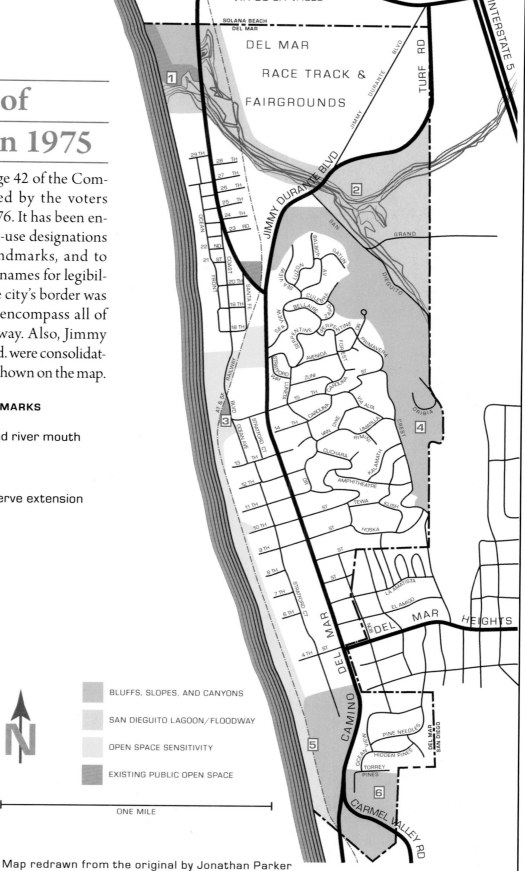

N

BLUFFS, SLOPES, AND CANYONS

SAN DIEGUITO LAGOON/FLOODWAY

OPEN SPACE SENSITIVITY

EXISTING PUBLIC OPEN SPACE

ONE MILE

Map redrawn from the original by Jonathan Parker

Book 1 Contents

Foreword—x

Preface—xiv

City of Del Mar in 1975 (map)—xvi

About Book 1—xvii

PART 1: Celebrations & Remembrances—1

🄟 The Way It Was—2
Celebrations & Remembrances

Introduction to Part 1—5

Gardner is a symbol of Del Mar *(11/27/82)*—7
Gardner Stevens

Joan's mark *(4/11/84)*—8
Joan Powers. Robert Frost quoted

The impossible dream *(5/5/84)*—9
J. David Dominelli. Man of La Mancha quoted

A tribute to Bill Healy *(1/23/85)*—10
Del Mar's long-time Planning Director leaves

The death of 481-SDLT? *(5/25/85)*—12
San Dieguito Little Theater. Dawn Mills

Joe and Ginny *(7/17/85)*—13
Joe and Ginny Harper

See no evil *(8/21/85)*—14
My 60th birthday

Of neighborhood barn-raisings and hog-killings *(2/5/86)*—15
Lew and Ruby Hopkins

He went about his business of living *(3/22/86)*—17
Bob Nelson

Saying goodbye to Milt *(7/12/86)*—18
Milt Smith. Thornton Wilder quoted

The guardian of the law *(3/14/87)*—20
Lisa Strandgaard, the new Planning Director

Remembering Madam Del Mar *(11/25/87)*—22
Nancy Ewing

Zel Camiel: He was a great person among us *(6/17/87)*—24
"Mayor" of the Plaza

Breaking ground into the future *(7/8/88)*—26
Jim Watkins and the Del Mar Inn

Del Mar's best women leaders *(11/30/88)*—27
Mayors, managers and directors. Helen Reddy quoted

Volunteer mayors of Del Mar *(5/5/89)*—28
From Tom Douglas to John Gillies

🄟 Tom Pearson's Exceptional Fortitude—29
Del Mar's Early Five-Term Mayor

Paul Lapolla, CRM, and the Del Mar that came to be *(6/2/89)*—30
Paul Lapolla and CRM. Theodore Roethke quoted

Keeping jazz alive in Del Mar *(7/26/89)*—31
Helen and Dayna entertain on Orchid Lane. Hadda Brooks quoted

The impossible dream revisited *(7/28/89)*—32
Nancy Hoover and the Dominelli affair. Man of La Mancha quoted

🄟 The J. David Affair—33
Too Good To Be True

Richard Carter and Tom Ranglas: Del Mar is more than voters *(8/4/89)*—34
Richard Carter and Tom Ranglas

Citizen Joe Shirley *(8/16/89)*—35
Downed at sea. Ralph Waldo Emerson quoted

Helen Drysdale: "Spaces" show at Channel 38 *(11/1/89)*—36
Photographer to the stars

McQuiston launches his boat *(11/15/89)*—37
His labor of love. Henry Thoreau quoted.

Joe and Janet Ream left large legacy *(1/27/90)*—38
Lost at sea

Robin Mitchell takes over helm at Chamber of Commerce *(2/9/90)*—39
Blessed with something beautiful

Anita Bingham: a class act *(3/14/90)*—41
A finance director proud of her work

Celebrating mothers at the Inn on Sunday *(5/11/90)*—42
Virginia Igonda's Ocean Song. Barbara Bush and Martin Buber quoted

Bob Curry leaves us with love *(5/25/90)*—43
Gloria's husband. Sammy Cahn and James Van Heusen quoted

Herb Turner: American regionalist *(6/20/90)*—45
Builder and artist

Kitty and Karl stirring memories of Del Mar *(7/18/90)*—47
Kitty and Karl Nicholasen, The Spectator. Esther Rich quoted.

🄟 Del Marriage—48
Kitty and Karl's Wedding

Arts Park and Richard Carter leave lasting echo (8/22/90)—**49**
Richard Carter

The two faces of Del Mar and a New Year's wish (12/26/90)—**51**
Zel Camiel, Janet and Joe Ream

David Furcolo has had his last word (1/9/91)—**52**
Seeker and free spirit. Big Elk, chief of the Omahas, quoted

Memoir to a great New York lady (4/17/91)—**53**
Betty Freedman Barson, mother of my children

Esther had fun and sought meaning (4/24/91)—**54**
Esther Rich Cherney

Del Mar residents fete Mother's Day (5/15/91)—**56**
Virginia Igonda

David and Brooke: a reflection (10/25/91)—**57**
David and Brooke Eisenberg. Margaret Fuller quoted

John Dunn: Phoenix rises from the ashes (12/6/91)—**58**
Sculptor survives the blaze

Gordon Denyes made Del Mar better (1/29/92)—**59**
A civic leader quietly building

Remembering Rosalind Lorwin (2/5/93)—**60**
Councilwoman and Mayor. Habits of the Heart quoted

Swede Throneson: Del Mar's historian (4/14/93)—**61**
Mr. Del Mar passes on

Ⓟ H. K. "Swede" & Marge Throneson—**62**
Collecting Del Mar's History

Lew and Ruby Hopkins set an example for all (6/24/94)—**63**
"Optimist Creed" quoted

Ⓟ Lew & Ruby Hopkins—**64**
Setting an Example for Service

Camiel one of Del Mar's great ladies (1/27/95)—**65**
Zel and Jeanne quoted

Camiel's letters chronicled Del Mar (12/1/95)—**66**
Jeanne's "one way" correspondence

Jorgensen's talents will be missed (5/3/95)—**67**
Del Mar's numbers cruncher will make music

PART 2: Del Mar Days—69

Ⓟ The Way It Was—**70**
Del Mar Days

Introduction to Part 2—**72**

25 years from now (7/11/84)—**73**
History and the 1930s WPA Guide to California

"Jewish Christmas" memories (12/22/82)—**75**
Back East in boyhood

Poetry and encroachments (7/20/83)—**76**
Library book sales. Edgar A. Guest quoted

Ars longa, vita brevis (11/2/83)—**77**
A trip to Tri City hospital in Oceanside

People and genial mayhem (1/25/84)—**78**
Chamber of Commerce dinner

Del Mar Days: the thrill of victory, the agony of the heat (9/19/84)—**80**
A mini-Olympics on the city streets and beach

Celebrating the miraculous (12/22/84)—**82**
The stories of Christmas and Hanukkah

Dialogue for '85: the wisdom of Mama Schwartz (12/29/84)—**83**
People wanting to be heard. Walt Whitman and Martin Buber quoted

Return of the Big Top (1/2/85)—**85**
Circus Vargas

Wildflower time and fixed ideas (3/2/85)—**86**
Putting aside politics for a walk on the bluffs

Small wisdoms and thinking of the best (3/16/85)—**87**
Optimist Club oratorical contest

Ⓟ Del Mar-Solana Beach Optimists—**88**
Friend of Youth

Del Mar fare (6/29/85)—**89**
Del Mar Fair and parade, Summer Sushi. Books of Isaiah and Genesis quoted

Echoes and visions (7/10/85)—**90**
Reflections on Del Mar history

Centennial chronicle (7/24/85)—**92**
Del Mar's Centennial celebration.

Splendid things (11/6/85)—**94**
Micky Benjamin and her boutique. Dayna Carroll lyrics quoted

Taking a night on the town (11/30/85)—**95**
Live performances at Channel 38

A visit to our neighborhood (1/4/86)—**96**
Fairbanks Ranch, Del Mar Highlands, Carmel Valley, Solana Beach, Cardiff

A trip around the countryside (1/8/86)—**97**
Carlsbad, Leucadia, Encinitas, Cardiff, Solana Beach

Happy New Year to us all (9/14/86)—**99**
The Jewish New Year, Judaism, my father, and Mark Twain

Our magical stage (10/1/86)—**100**
Musical entertainments in Del Mar

On fathers and forgiveness (10/8/86)—**101**
Ken Druck's workshop, "Alive and Male," my father, cousin, and uncle

Who really lives here? (10/25/86)—**102**
Comparing Del Mar and New York City

A gift for the new year (12/31/86)—**103**
Reflections on change

Hotdance: A time to harmonize (8/21/87)—**104**
Richard Carter's 5th Annual at the Arts Park

A time for settling old scores (12/23/88)—**106**
*Del Mar still scrapping as world comes together.
Robert Frost and Dylan Thomas quoted*

A day at the Del Mar races (2/15/89)—**107**
An appreciation of Del Mar's most famous institution

Children remind us of courage (5/24/89)—**108**
*Optimist Club Children's Challenge awards. Eleanor
Roosevelt quoted.*

A vote for Alvarado-Arballo (7/19/89)—**109**
Naming an historic Del Mar house. Nancy Ewing quoted

📷 The Alvarado House—*110*
Jacob Taylor Sells His First Del Mar Lot in 1885

Capturing the miracle of light (10/18/89)—**111**
*Joaquín Sorolla, "painter of light" exhibit. Book of
Genesis and Herb Turner quoted*

All's well in our town (11/8/89)—**112**
The first "Second Sunday in Del Mar" at the Inn

Hands across the border (11/10/89)—**113**
*Del Mar's Chamber of Commerce welcomes Tijuana's
Chamber*

More magic theater in Del Mar (11/29/89)—**114**
*Del Mar Theater Ensemble and Ensemble Arts Theater
launched*

Del Mar's real problem: no snow (12/15/89)—**115**
*Christmas celebration at Del Mar Inn. Dylan Thomas
quoted*

Southfair art: Male nudes provide a provocative exhibit
(12/20/89)—**116**
*New messages by two local artists. David Lewinson
quoted*

***Wilde Tales* delivers knockout of a show at the Plaza**
(2/28/90)—**117**
*Bonnie Tarwater's Theatre Ensemble brings Oscar Wilde
to life. Robertson Davies quoted*

Cowabunga! Celebration for Winston School at Sea World
(5/16/90)—**118**
Harnessing kid power in Del Mar

Family farce *Scapan* acts as a merry romp at Plaza
(7/11/90)—**119**
Del Mar Theater Ensemble. Moliere quoted

New traffic islands will change Stratford Court (7/20/90)—**120**
*A walking tour of the people, histories, and places on my
street*

Succos comes to Inn L'Auberge (10/12/90)—**121**
A Jewish harvest festival

**Channel 38 to hold Harvest Moon Auction and Autumn
Feast** (10/24/90)—**122**
Local-access TV comes of age

Auction stirs up TV memories of CTAC (11/7/90)—**123**
Local-access cable TV in Del Mar

***1940's Radio Hour* is holiday show** (11/23/90)—**125**
*Olive Blakistone's North Coast Rep revives voices of
the past*

Exploring Del Mar's beach and bluffs (1/4/91)—**126**
A walking tour

Council speaks up for Del Mar renters (5/24/91)—**127**
Jawboning a building owner

Del Mar is focus for computer arts (3/20/91)—**128**
*Bill Gladstone's first annual computer book publishing
forum*

Southfair opens Drysdale exhibit (6/14/91)—**129**
Herb Turner's Artists Space. John Ruskin quoted

DM Blues and Greens shaped city (12/27/91)—**130**
History of Del Mar's political factions

Reflections on a not-too-shabby place (2/12/92)—**131**
*Despite national politics, some of the benefits on the
local scene*

Holiday season a time for reflection (12/11/92)—**132**
Christmas in Woodstock. Dylan Thomas quoted

SCRAPBOOK: The Way It Was—*133*

Introduction to Scrapbook—*137*
📷 The Plaza: A Jewel in the Crown—*138*
📷 The Inn L'Auberge—*140*
📷 Thriving and Enterprising Community
Theaters—*142*
📷 Channel 37/38 Cable Provides a Stage—*144*
📷 Richard Carter and the Arts Park—*146*
📷 A Center for Publishers, Editors and Designers—*148*
📷 The Restaurateurs—*150*
📷 Nancy Ewing: Madam Del Mar—*152*
📷 Don McQuiston—*154*
📷 Herb Turner—*156*
📷 "Helen"—H. Montgomery-Drysdale—*158*
📷 Alice Goodkind—*160*
📷 Where the Surf Meets the Turf—*162*
📷 The Canyon and the Lagoon—*164*

Index—*167*

DEL MAR 1983

A Sharp Design/Jone Dupre Illustrator

DEL MAR DAYS OCTOBER 1 & 2

Sponsored by the Del Mar Foundation

The Del Mar Foundation, founded in 1982 at Lou Terrell's initiative, hosted scores of street and beach events for Del Mar Days weekend, including a triathlon and 25-mile bike race that attracted wide interest and brought sufficient crowds onto the Del Mar streets for the event eventually to be discontinued. Through the years the Foundation has sponsored concerts in the Park, events at the Powerhouse, and financial support for worthy projects in the city.

www.delmarfoundation.org

Reproduced with permission of JoAnn Sharp

A Gallery of People, Events & Places

How to bring alive an experience not so long gone, but yet long enough to play with memory, with its subtle oversights and alterations? In this scrapbook I have chosen some of the people, events, and aspects of my first-hand experience that stand out most in my memory. They do not at all pretend to reflect all of what was going on, nor all among us who were shaping events or keeping our civic life alive and well. Nonetheless, they are of a vitality and a reservoir of talent, enterprise, and optimism whose qualities I think most of us who were present at the moment shared in our own way. Below is a pictorial table of contents.

The Plaza

PAGE
138

The new Plaza opened in 1989. Ivan Gayler (*left*) and David Winkler breathed new life into downtown after winning a vigorously fought referendum.

The Inn L'Auberge

PAGE
140

Jim Watkins's Tudor building style is seen all over town. Shown here with wife Carol (*right*) and daughter K. C. at 1988 groundbreaking of the new hotel.

Community Theaters

PAGE
142

The mid-1980s found the area with four prolific repertory theaters filling seats with the gamut of classic to contemporary, expressively directed.

Del Mar Local Cable

PAGE
144

Daniels Cablevision won a vigorous 1981 franchise contest. Vacation resident Bill Daniels, the "father of cable," financed a state-of-the-art studio.

Richard Carter

PAGE
146

Our hometown impressario, seen at right with Mary Hale, Del Mar's ubiquitous events MC, livened Camino for a decade with performance-art events, creating the Zinn Building Arts Park.

The Publishers

PAGE
148

Employing over 300 professionals in its 1967–77 heyday, *Psychology Today* spawned a nationally renowned innnovative publishing and design center in and around Del Mar.

The Restaurateurs

PAGE 150

The restaurateurs of Del Mar provided residents and visitors alike with good meals, social centers, great views, and memorable Sundowners and Happy Hours.

Nancy Ewing

PAGE 152

Nancy Ewing, my best friend before she passed in 1987, was an astute columnizing observer of the local scene. She was adopted as Madam Del Mar, and authored the coffee-table history *Del Mar: Looking Back*.

Don McQuiston

PAGE 154

Don McQuiston's work epitomized the elegance of design and book-making that characterized our prolific graphic design community.

Herb Turner

PAGE 156

Turner, citizen artist and builder, produced more than 60 Del Mar residences, several major developments, and a body of fine art. He was a self-defined regionalist and environmental designer.

H. Montgomery-Drysdale

PAGE 158

Unobtrusive behind her camera, Drysdale produced a huge body of striking black-and-white celebrity and Americana images, venturing cross-country and abroad from her Del Mar home base.

Alice Goodkind

PAGE 160

An accomplished violinist, artist, and humorist, Alice was a passionate nature lover, who was a founder of the Friends of the San Dieguito Lagoon and a leader in the Lagoon's preservation.

Track & Shore

PAGE 162

"Where the turf meets the surf," Bing Crosby's memorable description of Del Mar as a vacation spot and recreation area, still rings true.

Canyons & Lagoon

PAGE 164

A strong commitment to environmental preservation by Del Mar residents has defended precious land forms and habitats from the surrounding and enveloping San Diego urban mass.

About Book 2

The three parts in **Book 2** are unified by themes of individual and community rights, public policy, and constitutional liberties, as they emerged in the course of local civic engagement.

When I first arrived in 1969 from New York City to the coast of North County San Diego, one could see mostly undeveloped chaparral-dotted mesas, sandstone canyons, and rural towns to the east. They were already on the drawing boards in the early 1970s to become what is now a completely developed, landscaped, and paved-over region, separated from a Del Mar "eden" on the west by 13 or more merging north-south lanes of Interstates 5 and 805.

The 43 of my columns that appear in **Part 3** deal with the battles over property rights and environmental issues that eventually settled the city's character through referendum and regulation. These contests arose between factions polarized on issues of land-use regulation and building design in the larger region as well as in the city's 1.8-square-mile jurisdiction.

Some of the global and national issues that filtered into Del Mar's public life appear in **Part 4**. Its 35 columns embrace the era of the first Gulf War, flag-burning protests, removing Santa from the classroom, the fatwa against author Salman Rushdie, the collapse of the Soviet Union, and U. S. Immigration Service sweeps of buses and businesses, and roundups of what were known then as "illegals"—mainly young Mexicans who walked up from Baja along the coast, working the farms and yards in the area.

Water-use policy and waste disposal were also critical county-wide, as well as being local concerns.

In the 42 columns of **Part 5**, I drew connections about the moral, ethical, legal, and social underpinnings of our society. I quoted from historic documents (cited in the "Bibliography and Commentary" section of **Book 3**), dealing with political factions, free speech, religious liberty, church and state, property rights, civic engagement, and local government.

Looking back, I notice in **Part 5** and elsewhere, occasions that bring out local expressions of patriotism and honor to the flag in the community.

Articulate and informed debate seemed to come naturally to our population, 60% of whom (according to the Census) were employed in education, management, and other professions. The fundamentals of this debate appear to me to be universal in the five exchanges voiced in local newspapers that I have selected for the **Afterword:** How can we reconcile individual liberty and democracy? How and when can adversaries join forces for the common good? What are the proper standards of public discourse? What is the civic social contract? What interests drive the local agenda?

In the course of the 23 years from 1969 through 1992, when I first lived, worked, or did business in the City of Del Mar, I became so bonded to its civic life and ethos that it overtook the Bronx, where I was raised as a boy, as my primary spiritual home base. My sponsoring newspapers, the *Surfcomber* and the *Blade-Citizen*, gave me a front-page send-off, reproduced here in the **Epilog**, when I went east in 1992. My friends in Del Mar organized a farewell event in Seagrove Park. It brought out supporter and adversary alike.

Who is to say what we sow with our works? How could I know that I would return again in 2012?

Book 2 Contents

Overview: Books 1, 2 & 3—*x*

About Book 2—*xvi*

PART 3: On Land & Its Uses—*173*

ⓟ The Way It Was—174
On Land and Its Uses

Introduction to Part 3—177

Does anybody love a wall? (8/10/83)—179
A sea wall for Del Mar. Robert Frost quoted

Waves of indignation…yours and ours (12/17/83)—180
Aftermath of the storm and the sand budget.
Stephen crane quoted

Discovering what it was all about (4/1/84)—182
Jim Tetrault and the new Council

Council tying up loose ends (4/21/84)—183
New Council considers new plans

Holding developers hostage (9/15/84)—184
Owner rights and "the price of admission"

Common sense should guide differing factions (1/19/85)—186
Environmentalists and limited government.
Marianne Moore quoted

Life after Bill Healy (1/26/85)—187
Planning Director controlled land-use agenda

Beach issues and solutions (12/18/85)—188
Beach issue history. Rousseau quoted

More beach history (12/28/85)—190
Committees, Jim Scripps, and BOZO
(beach overlay zone)

Carsten and Dougherty—A vote for the future (4/2/86)—191
Outcomes of the candidates forum

The new spirit of '86 (8/23/86)—192
Reawakening as a community with common values?

Barney builds a dream house (3/24/89)—194
A Del Mar resident tries to get his house plans approved
(Part 1 of a series)

Eighth Street protection area (3/29/89)—195
Neighbors on the block try to protect view corridor
(Part 2)

The last one in is a rotten... (3/31/89)—197
People who enjoy views don't always want to share
(Part 3)

A visit to the Hall of Justice (4/5/89)—199
Barney didn't get his house—the Council said no (Part 4)

How sweet the Plaza really is (4/12/89)—200
Ivan Gayler and David Winkler. Carl Sandberg quoted

On legislating bookstores (6/7/89)—201
Town considers permitting another bookstore

Singing the praises of the Inn (8/2/89)—203
Jim and Carol Watkins and the Inn opening

ⓟ Jim & Carol Watkins—204
Renewing Del Mar in the 1970s

Is justice denied in Del Mar? (9/6/89)—205
Catch-22 in getting approvals in Del Mar

Design by committee flourishes (1/12/90)—207
The cost of getting an awning design approved

Permit process should get overhaul in Del Mar (3/16/90)—208
The cost complexity and length of time it takes

Join the Lagoon Cleanup (3/21/90)—209
Preserving the marvels of a vibrant habitat

Del Mar DRB vs. flower stand (7/27/90)—211
Design Review Board turns down a popular awning

Del Mar to be ruled by coastal plan (8/3/90)—212
City will lose, gain autonomy when plan goes to
Coastal Commission

Countdown on Local Coastal Plan (8/17/90)—213
Plan will override local land use rules

ⓟ Jan McMillan—215
Conscience of Del Mar

DRB an easy target (8/29/90)—216
How design review works (Part 1 of a series)

Design Review Board works well (8/31/90)—218
Examples of workaday problem-solving (Part 2)

DRB often infuriates, tackles tough issues (9/5/90)—219
Controversy and contradictions go with the job (Part 3)

Design review needs redesign (9/7/90)—220
System's uncertainties, complexities need revision (Part 4)

As population drops, economy grows (2/6/91)—222
Del Mar's demographics and economics

One more victim of DM review process (3/8/91)—223
A young couple's efforts to replace an old home
with a new one

DM reverses house decision (3/27/91)—224
How local politics works in the review process

Rules needed but still confound (5/29/91)—226
The need to come up with workable rules

On regional development (6/21/91)—**227**
Balancing development, environmental needs.
The Experience of Place quoted

Three years yields a house no one wants (7/17/91)—**228**
Everyone loses when an owner's efforts are foiled
at every turn

Coastal plan highlights U. S. wetlands dilemma (9/6/9 1)—**230**
A Del Mar drainage ditch and andy berm become
wetlands

Judge hands Del Mar lesson in basic civics (8/30/91)—**231**
Injunction is issued to delay controversial traffic- control-
device program

Some Del Mar residents fear condominium-izing
(10/11/91)—**232**
Zoning loophole defeats intended neighborhood character

The dilemma of vanishing forests (10/23/91)—**233**
Richard Manning's Last Stand reveals forest devastation

Whether we like it or not, man is in charge of nature
(2/14/92)—**234**
Daniel Botkin's Discordant Harmonies: Man decides
which environment to preserve

Zoning laws help define a city (10/6 /93)—**235**
The future of Del Mar. James Kunstler's The Geography
of Nowhere quoted

PART 4: Public Policy & the Neighborhood—237

The Way It Was—**238**
Public Policy & the Neighborhood

Introduction to Part 4—**240**

We can make a difference (12/2/83)—**243**
Reflections on the prospect of nuclear war

Must we ban Santa Claus? (12/14/83)—**245**
Make-believe fun seems to be taken out of
the holiday season in our schools

High noon at Seagrove (1/4/84)—**247**
Peace Assembly at Seagrove Park

The new put-down (8/84)—**249**
Partisan politics, liberals and conservatives in Del Mar

This place of ours (10/10/84)—**251**
Two exhibits celebrate Jewish Holocaust history and survival.
Emma Lazarus, Gwendolyn Brooks quoted

Abduction (6/25/85)—**253**
Immigration Service picks up flower lady's
elementary-school apprentice

Visiting the river of our survival (10/9/85)—**255**
Del Mar's water travels from the Colorado River.
Hart Crane quoted

Quality of life (6/28/86)—**256**
Conversation with Herb Turner on life in our town

A matter of life itself (12/3/86)—**257**
People I know who died of smoking and the proposed
no-smoking ordinance.

Dick Roe—**259**
Citizen Publisher

Between man and man (12/17/86)—**260**
Mayor Hopkins and Fair Board President square off.
Book of Proverbs, Buber, and Mama Schwartz quoted

Freedom rings clear and true in Del Mar (9/23/87)—**261**
Constitution's 200th anniversary celebrated
at Del Mar Heights School

On smokestacks and book burnings (3/8/89)—**262**
The Salman Rushdie controversy and local freedoms

Time to remember Holocaust (5/3/89)—**263**
Some history and the purpose of remembering
Golda Meir quoted

Life from a global perspective (6/16/89)—**264**
Del Martians Dr. Harold Bloomfield and
Sirah Vettese write about relationships

Free press speaks for everyone (7/14/89)—**265**
Writer, editor, and basic freedoms. Jefferson quoted

Mayor overreacts and teaches us a lesson (1/17/90)—**266**
Friends of Library newsletter riles mayor
Emerson quoted on quoting

Living inside Del Mar's mysteries (4/27/90)—**267**
The adventure of factions sharing the same mysteries.
Ray Bradbury quoted

DM schools top choice (9/12/90)—**268**
Superintendent runs a "meat and potatoes" operation.
Brookings report quoted

Much wasted energy in DM's conflicts (12/12/90)—**269**
Benefits of conflict management. Western City quoted

Peace and goodwill are not easy to come by in time of
Mideast crisis (12/21/90)—**270**
Why is mideast peace taking so long? Anwar Sadat and
Charles Dickens quoted

Thoughts on somber night of January 15 (1/18/91)—**271**
Mideast crisis captures Del Mar's attention. Stephen
Crane quoted

More thoughts on why we are at war again (1/23/91)—**272**
Gulf War has displaced local issues

Faxes from Jerusalem: the sky war (2/13/91)—**273**
What would it be like to be in Jerusalem? (Part 1 of 2)

Scuds over DM: How would we feel? (2/15/91) —**274**
More from my friend in Israel. Some Muslim history.
(Part 2 of 2)

Lessons for DM on setting its goals *(3/1/91)*—**275**
Drawing from Gulf War on goal setting. Leadership Is an Art and The Art of War quoted

When is policy a moral issue? *(5/31/91)*—**277**
It is moral to pursue special interest. Habits of the Heart quoted

BOZO leaves a bad line at Jake's beach frontage *(5/8/91)*—**278**
Beach preservation initiative said to disregard history

BOZO oversight should be fixed by the City *(5/10/91)*—**279**
Sloppy documentation yields the wrong map line. Bud Emerson's response

DM eatery's BOZO line is rights issue *(6/12/91)*—**281**
Drawing an arbitrary beach overlay line took property. William Penn quoted

Police need to have the public's trust *(7/10/91)*—**282**
Police seem too quick to shoot. League of California Cities quoted

Collapse of Soviet Union offers new hope to world *(9/4/91)*—**283**
People of Eastern European origin deeply moved by Soviet collapse.

Pressure on schools for new approaches *(10/18/91)*—**285**
Checking out local schools and national trends

A time for good words and neighborly peace *(12/4/91)*—**286**
Israelis and Palestinians sit down together. Book of Proverbs, Shamir, and Shafi quoted

Christmas, crosses won't harm us *(12/18/91)*—**288**
No harm in recognizing mainstream culture. Charles Dickens quoted

PART 5: The Individual, Liberty & Community—*291*

Ⓟ The Way It Was—*292*
The Individual, Liberty & Community

Introduction to Part 5—294

Legislative tyranny *(10/12/83)*—**297**
Trying to force a high-speed bullet train through

Right track, wrong signals *(5/14/84)*—**298**
Late-night city council meetings stir suspicions of secrecy

Current city politics *(10/31/84)*—**299**
Attitudes towards government and leadership. The business of ideas.

Limits of government *(11/3/84)*—**301**
When must government act, and when is it optional or wrong to act at all?

Storm in a chalice *(12/5/84)*—**302**
The mayor runs a prayer breakfast: religion and government. Bible quoted

Idea power *(7/20/85)*—**303**
Community planning and marketplace choices. Lewis Mumford quoted

Del Mar dialogue *(11/16/85)*—**305**
Reflections on the cancelled Mira Costa College debate, "Peace with Justice in the Middle East." William Penn quoted

A promenade for Del Mar? *(1/29/86)*—**306**
UCSD's Helen and Newton Harrison harness the currents of community.

Power to the people *(4/12/86)*—**307**
"The people are always right"—my side in the recent city elections gets thoroughly shellacked.

Men – and women – of words *(8/6/86)*—**308**
The revolutionary power of words. Eric Hoffer, Thoreau quoted

A case of elitism? *(9/17/86)*—**310**
Some small towns try to keep people out. Elitism?

Of government and local politics *(2/7/87)*—**311**
Cities, thought to be unstable, cradle our liberties. Hamilton quoted

Ⓟ Pat Barnett—*312*
Civic Engagement by Design

The hanging town *(3/4/87)*—**313**
The rule of law, passion of the moment and sense of proportion. Melville quoted

The new American revolution *(4/25/87)*—**314**
Part 1—Nation is looking for a new sense of community values. Hillel quoted

Where we stand in Del Mar *(5/1/87)*—**316**
Part 2—Del Mar needs a new vocabulary to discuss change . Habits of the Heart quoted

If not now, when? *(5/20/87)*—**317**
Part 3—The basic question: individualism vs. community. Habits of the Heart quoted

Hardball - Del Mar style *(8/12/88)*—**318**
Hardball as a metaphor for the political game.

Del Mar adversaries share a civic commitment *(9/16/88)*—**320**
Resemblances in roles among adversaries in town. I.F. Stone quoted

Flag, God and country *(10/11/88)*
Jean Neville's passing and the Bush-Dukakis campaign.

A Time to test our liberties *(7/7/89)*—**322**
Recent Supreme Court rulings on flag burning and abortion. Roscoe Pound quoted

Where was the community? *(8/11/89)*—**323**
Planning of new city center will fail if not all elements of community participate. Habits of the Heart quoted

Is it divisive to label factions? *(11/24/89)*—**324**
*Part 1—Faction labels in local politics serve a useful
purpose. James Madison quoted.*

Who are the Blues and Greens? *(12/1/89)*—**325**
*Part 2—Factions in Del Mar identified (Part 2 of a
series). De Tocqueville quoted.*

Turning factions to good use *(12/8/89)*—**326**
*Part 3—Factions operating in the open can be Helpful.
Voltaire quoted.*

"Memorandum" has message for us *(2/14/90)*—**328**
*North Coast Repertory Theatre presents
Vacklav Havel's satire on the heavy hand of bureaucracy*

Del Mar's sixth Council member *(7/13/90)*—**329**
Piero Ariotti keeps watch over the rules

Thanksgiving day: a time to celebrate community
(11/21/90)—**330**
*Home base is worth fighting for.
Lydia Child, Robert Frost quoted*

U.S. a cradle for ideals of liberty *(7/3/91)*—**332**
*A trip to Washington, D. C. and Concord,
Massachusetts rich with reminders of the wellsprings of
American ideas of liberty and their origins in Western
civilization*

Thomas hearings test definitions of rights *(10/4/91)*—**333**
*Natural law, common law, and constitutional
law discussed*

Thomas hearings prompt reflections on the truth
(11/20/91)—**334**
*How can we know the truth of a matter?
Will Rogers quoted*

Del Mar should learn the art of negotiation *(2/21/92)*—**336**
Alternatives to "gotcha-got 'em" politics

DM residents clash over rights *(2/26/92)*—**337**
Conflict between "community" and "individual" rights

Somewhere there's a common ground *(2/28/92)*—**338**
*Common interests and issues surround local conflicts.
Last column before leaving for Woodstock, New York*

He's taking stock in Woodstock *(3/27/92)*—**339**
Life in Woodstock, New York

Small-town ideal is our nation's life blood *(7/10/92)*—**340**
*Contrasts and similarities between Del Mar
and Woodstock*

Del Mar had its own version of Perot *(8/7/92)*—**341**
Comparing Mayor Jim Tetrault with Ross Perot

Towns are centered by libraries *(10/4/92)*—**342**
Woodstock, Del Mar, and the Carnegie libraries

Cable channel important resource *(11/27/92)*—**344**
Local access cable in Del Mar and in Woodstock

Holiday season time for reflection *(12/11/92)*—**345**
*Christmas in Woodstock. Dylan Thomas and Tony Hiss
quoted.*

Del Mar must learn how to cut spending *(7/9/93)*—**346**
Woodstock and Del Mar budgets compared

Del Mar must adjust to circumstances *(11/12/93)*—**348**
Financing a new library for Del Mar

Labels getting in the way of good governance *(3/18/94)*—**349**
Del Mar's "Greens" and "Grays"

Gray vs. Green Debate only clouds the issues *(5/20/94)*—**350**
Assessing election results and Del Mar's political split

Small towns must retain identities *(1/14/94)*—**351**
Local "watchdogs" in Woodstock and Del Mar

AFTERWORD:
Looking Back on Our Big Debates—353

🖝 The Way It Was—354
Looking Back on Our Big Debates

Introduction to Afterword—**356**

1. Downtown Initiative: How can we reconcile liberty with democracy? *Surfcomber (10/2/85)*: The Downtown Initiative—359

"Reasons for an Initiative," by Deborah Isaacson (10/2/85)—**360**
We wish to vote on major developments that affect our daily lives.

"A Constitutional Issue," by Gene Schwartz (10/2/85)—**361**
Mighty constitutional underpinnings support the mundane concerns of local government.

Response by Ivo Feierabend (10/16/85)—**362**
An exercise in intellectualized insults

2. Planning Del Mar: How and when can adversaries join forces for the common good? *Surfcomber (7/30/86)*: Planning Del Mar's Future—363

"Del Mar Wish Lists," by Bud Emerson—**365**
A wonderful opportunity for bold leadership...a way to rise above politics

"Endangered Species," by Gene Schwartz—**366**
We should be commissioning the best private regional planning and transit talent

3. What are proper standards of public discourse? *Surfcomber (2/86)*: Be Careful What You Say—367

"The New Big Lie" by Gene Schwartz (2/26/86)—**368**
It has now become fashionable in Del Mar politics to completely rewrite history.

"An Adage to Remember: Never Call Somebody a Liar" by Jan McMillan (3/5/86)—**370**
It is rhetoric like this that poisons the air and scars the community for years afterwards.

"What's in a Word" by Gene Schwartz (5/7/86)—**371**
Defining the terms of the discourse could be helpful.

4. Individualism and Community: How do we strike a balance between the two? *North County Blade-Citizen (5/87)*—373

"If not now, when?" by Gene Schwartz (5/20/87)—**374**
Self-interest versus community interest. Habits of the Heart by Robert Bellah quoted

"Gene Schwartz gets Bellah wrong" by Gordon Clanton (6/3/87)—**375**
The political preference of Bellah and (Ayn) Rand are roughly 180 degrees apart.

"More on Bellah vs Rand," by Gene Schwartz (6/24/87)—**377**
Similar observations by Bellah and Rand on the dilemma of moral relativism

5. Partisan Politics in Del Mar: What interests drive the local agenda? *North County Blade-Citizen (5/91)*—379

"DM: a city run by special interests," by Gene Schwartz (5/1/91)—**381**
Special interest is the driving force of all human organisms. Charles Evans Hughes quoted.

"Debating the common good," by Gordon Clanton (5/10/91)—**383**
Gene reflects the libertarian view that there is no such thing as "the common good."

6. The Eye of the Beholder *Surfcomber (3/12/86)*—385
Three letters to the editor, from S. Gill Williamson, Dave Furcolo and Cathy Wood, responding to my column of 3/5/86 supporting Carsten and Dougherty for election to the City Council

EPILOG: Leaving Del Mar—387

🖝 The Way It Was—388
Leaving Del Mar

Introduction to Epilog—**390**

"Columnist heads for Woodstock" by Liz Swain, *Surfcomber* (2/19/92)—**391**

"Gene Schwartz leaving Del Mar for New York" by Shannon Strybel, *North County Blade-Citizen* (2/20/92)—**392**

"The caterpillar and the ant" by Gene Schwartz (12/28/1982)—**393**

Index—**395**

Designed for the Del Mar Foundation by Sharp Design. Reproduced with permission of JoAnn Sharp

About Book 3

My original plan was for two short paperbacks in a set that would cover some 200 of the more than 600 columns I wrote first for the *Del Mar Surfcomber* and then for the *North County Blade-Citizen*.

Because so many of the columns in **Book 2** referred to land use, zoning, and planning issues, over which we debated long and hard (the Del Mar civic center debate and development, for example, at this writing in the summer of 2015 is into its 30th year), I believed it would be useful to include some of the original documents for reference.

This also served my intention to record the history of those times as a case study in civic engagement. For those few who enjoy getting into the thick of it, it is instructive to see the ways in which a community such as Del Mar sought to preserve a broad vision by attending to its minutest details. (For example, when does a trellis contribute to floor area and when does it not? And what kind of design is compatible with that of the neighborhood?).

On the broader scale, what is the vision that animates the land-use and design criteria for the more than 30 zoning districts that define this 1.8-square-mile village? Del Mar has a 2-mile beachfront, a major racetrack, a floodplain and lagoon, bluffs, canyons, protected ecosystems. and 24/7 commuter, Amtrak and freight railroad service that passes through. Also some 2,200 dwelling units, 4,000 to 5,000 residents, and several hundred business enterprises. Del Mar's effective "downtown" commercial district is about six blocks north to south. The passionate feelings expressed for both development and preservation of the character of the community, each a gleam in the eye of a dreamer, come together in "City of Dreams," the theme of **Book 3**.

Part 6 documents a series of nine benchmarks that help to define Del Mar's vision. And nine additional newspaper columns accompany these entries.

Putting together this volume was also a process of discovery for me, when it became clear, as shown in the opening pages of **Part 6**, that the original dreams of Del Mar as a resort and vacation community, and a brief passage as an arts and publishing center (see the "Scrapbook" in **Book 1**), gave way to the primacy of the residential village it had become, and to the preservation of the wondrous natural habitat of which we are the custodians.

It is hard to believe that the internet as we know it did not exist in those years. Now, all of this documentation can be accessed on the city's interactive and real-time-updated website http://www.delmar.ca.us/.

No work of this nature can be truly useful unless it is well indexed. **Books 1 and 2** are provided with their own individual tables of contents and indexes. Book 3 provides a Combined List of Columns with the columns from all three volumes organized in a single chronological list, and a Combined Index for **Books 1, 2 & 3**.

Central to many of the broader questions I addressed in my columns, were the references I drew on to illustrate or reinforce my thoughts. Hence I have included in **Book 3** a "Bibliography and Commentary" with expanded notes about the works I consulted. Finally, I have included some "Source Notes: Illustrations and Citations," and "Acknowledgments" to those who have helped and encouraged me during the 23 years this work has been incubating.

Book 3 Contents

Overview: Books 1, 2 & 3—*x*

About Book 3—*xvii*

PART 6- City of Dreams—*401*

ⓟ The Way It Was—*402*
City of Dreams / The Rise of the Habitat

Introduction to Part 6—*404*

1. Cityhood Reconsidered & the 1960 Master Plan—*407*
Introduction and Commentary

The Del Mar Question: Consolidation or Incorporation *(1/22/70)*—*409*
Del Mar Surfcomber excerpts

The 1960 Del Mar City Charter—*411*

2. The Community Plan *(1975)*—*414*
Introduction and commentary

Excerpts from the 1976 Community Plan—*415*

3. The San Dieguito Lagoon Resource Enhancement Program *(1979)*—*441*
Introduction and commentary

Excerpts from the Program—*443*

4. Del Mar 2000 *(1981)*—*469*
Introduction and Commentary

Building on Del Mar 2000 *(9/21/83)*—*471*

ⓟ Bud Emerson—*472*
Challenging Del Mar to fulfill its dream

Excerpts from the report—*473*

5. The Library and Civic Center Master Plan *(1990–92)*—*507*

Introduction and commentary

The 1992 Special Election—*509*
Text of propositions and illustrations of plan presented to voters

Del Mar Community Center Master Plan.
(April 1990 excerpts)—*511*

DM Center nears completion *(5/22/91)*—*517*

Del Mar voters should OK community center *(1/3/92)*—*519*

Del Mar's leadership blew Center election *(1/31/92)*—*521*

6. The Local Coastal Land-Use Plan *(1993)*—*523*
Introduction and commentary

LCP is community plan revision *(9/14/90)*—*525*

Council to revew LCP in final draft *(1/25/91)*—*527*

Excerpts from Land-Use Plan certified by the California Coastal Commission, March 18, 1993—*529*

7. The Garden Del Mar *(2008)*—*547*
Introduction and commentary. Ballot argument favoring the referendum.

Excerpts from the Specific Plan adopted by the voters November 4, 2008—*549*

8. Design Review & Floor-Area Ratio *(1967–1992)*—*565*
Introduction and origins of the ordinances

DRB and Del Mar City Council tackle local permit process *(5/3/ 91)*—*567*

Current Ordinance and c.1992 comparison—*569*

Current FAR ordinance—*577*

9. The Ties that Bind: Del Mar & Its Railroad *(1882 to the present)*—*585*
Introduction: How the railroad came to Del Mar

Proposal to Retain Limited Services at the Del Mar Station—*587*

Excerpts from proposal submitted by the City of Del Mar, February, 1990—*589*

BACK OF THE BOOK—*595*

ⓟ Hotdance 1990—*596*

Bibliography and Commentary—*597*

Acknowledgments—*607*

Source Notes: Illustrations and Citations—*608*

ⓟ Triathlon 1981—*609*

Chronological Combined List of Columns—*610*

ⓟ Innovations—Published! 1970—*618*

Index—*619*

KEEP GREENERY IN THE SCENERY

Support the Del Mar Park Preserve Plan, an opportunity to share in a unique effort to protect and preserve our home environment.

Poster designed in 1972 by Don McQuiston for Seagrove Park and Del Mar Bluff Preservation fund-raising campaign. Illustration by John Dawson. See page 52 of *Del Mar: Looking Back* by Nancy Ewing for more about the campaign.

Made in the USA
San Bernardino, CA
09 November 2016